Phases: Poems

Tayler Simon

Published by Tayler Simon, 2023.

PHASES: POEMS

First edition. October 31, 2023.

Copyright © 2023 Tayler Simon.

ISBN: 979-8223200420

Written by Tayler Simon.

Table of Contents

For the people who saw me through this journey and loved me anyway

For all the people going through their own phases

Preface

In my eleventh-grade English class, we did many unconventional things for an AP Language class. One of those assignments felt right out of a feel-good family film with a savior complex set in an inner-city high school classroom. It took me a minute to dig through my old journals to find my "Porait Poem" or my "I am" poem. I open this collection of poetry with this poem because that is who I thought I was at the time, and it serves as a reminder that I will never be the same and will always be the same.

As I was looking through those old journals from the beginning of the pandemic in 2020, I saw that I was a poet, even beyond the terrible angsty poems I had written in high school before 2012. I got to see my journey through the years and how far I had come. I went from thinking I could only thrive in the shadows to looking forward to bathing in the light.

Phases is a peek into that journey of self-discovery. This work is a love letter to who I used to be (who I can still be at times) and how she helped me survive to get to where I am now. I struggled in the past with feeling that I was unseen, that I would never be understood. Vulnerability tends to be difficult for me, and publishing my deep innermost thoughts and feelings– especially under my real name– is the ultimate test of vulnerability, a love offering to my younger self who wanted to be seen.

I hope you, dear reader, find something you can connect to in these poems. I hope this can be an encouragement for you to start or continue your own journey to find yourself, be unapologetically vulnerable, and love on the parts of you that feel unloveable.

A BURDEN

Portrait Poem (2012)

I am a nerdy romantic
I wonder if I am capable of receiving love
I hear the cries of the lonely
I see all of the warmth of the love
From the people who don't exist
I just want to know if I can love
I am a nerdy romantic

I pretend to be an optimist
I feel the indifference my father has instilled in me
I touch the phantom hands of God trying to guide me
I worry I will disappoint
I cry for the unhappiness of everyone
I am a nerdy romantic

I understand how not to understand
I say that I am happy
I dream of love one day
I try to do my best
I hope to finally get what I want
I am a nerdy romantic

I love myself when I feel skinny
I love myself when I feel accomplished
I love myself when people show me
How much they love me

   - conditional

They say you can't feel
if someone licks your elbow
You move around life unfeeling
taking licks to your elbow
pretending it's not there
Knowing if you allowed yourself
to feel the pain
it's anything but funny

 - funny bone

Feelings aren't real
Nightmares aren't either
But they are to me
in the moment

   - bedtime prayers

How can I be
too much
and not enough
at the same time?

- *paradox*

They tell me feelings
are a burden
just something
to get in the way
I should disconnect
from other people
and wither in isolation
pretending that
everything is ok
and I'm the only one
going through storms

- the only one

I'm watching the shadows
dance across the wall
There's a warmth in my belly
tequila again
The opposite of full
is empty
There's a tightness in my throat
more tequila
to wash it down

I don't have a problem
do I?

- liquid (dis)courage

What is the difference
between want and need?

Why can't I want
the things that I need?

How can I stop
needing what I want?

- maslow

There are so many different flavors of sad
There's grief, hopelessness, loneliness
There's deprivation, isolation (real or self-inflicted)
There's pain, there's regret

Love can make you sad
Hate can make you sad
Fear can make you sad

   - 32 flavors

There is a tiny ball in my chest,
threatening to seize hold of my very being.
I'm a human doing with no time for being.
My spirit is dying and I feel guilty
for not wanting to keep poisoning it more.
Productivity and hegemony over everything.

The ball is getting bigger.
Head scratching.
Fist clenching.
Cold chills down my spine.

I can't do this.
I can't do this.
I can't do this.

People who break down are broken.
Worthless.

    - in my body

Anxiety feels like
I'm going to swallow
my whole self through
my own throat

Anxiety feels like
the rising water in the sink
right before you turn on
the garbage disposal

Anxiety feels like
an underwater contest
except not for
fun with friends

Anxiety feels like
straining for something
just outside of
your desperate reach

Anxiety feels like
not being spotted
while bench pressing
and dropping the weight

Anxiety feels like
going on a
ten-mile run
in the southern heat

  - anxiety feels like I

But anxiety also feels like
walking into a room
and totally forgetting
why you went in there

Anxiety also feels like
getting stopped
at every red light
when you're running late

Anxiety also feels like
Waking during
Sleep paralysis
With the witch on your chest

Anxiety also feels like
trying to remember
to go left or right
at the fork in the road

Anxiety also feels like
waiting for lab results
and pulling the jenga block
and sinking into quicksand

- anxiety feels like too

I am softness
I am both warm on one side
and cold on the other

I would rather be over there
I am part of a rotation
interchangeable

I dream of being clean again
I am worried about losing my shape
becoming stiff

I want to be wanted for my comfort
I am alive at night
waiting to serve my purpose

The best thing I've done
is catch your tears

The worst thing I've done
was try to smother you

I am guilty of not being enough
to block out the world

I live for the time of night
where you and I meet

The point of my life is
to hold your head

I want to be remembered
for you always coming home to me

- pillow

Can we stop wasting our time
comparing your gunshot wounds
to my stab wound?
Because in the end
we're both bleeding out
and I want us
to heal together

    - insignificant

I want to crawl
out of my skin
I want to hurt
myself with more feelings

Shoot me
Stone me
Tear off my flesh
Let me bleed out
on the concrete

Keep coming feelings
drown me in a teal sea
I want to feel it all
not escape

    - gimme gimme more

PERFECTION

19

If no one sees
my imperfections
do they really
exist?

    - a tree falls

There are starving children in Africa
So I must be grateful for all I have
Take all that I am offered
Thank you
Yes, I'll take more

It's impolite to turn down an offering
It's rude to leave anything behind
Because you just never know
when your next meal is coming

So keep eating
until you're sick
until you're bursting

There is an insatiable hole
you are trying to fill
with the wrong things

   - more please

I need all these extras
just to feel normal
What is normal anyway?
I am not normal
but I want weird
not dysfunctional

    - *spicy*

My walls stay up to protect me
until I get back to the safety
of myself

   - armor

I felt so alone
because I couldn't find
people I could
connect to
as my true self
because I didn't know
who she was
And I didn't care to know
who she was
because I was too busy
trying to shape myself
into what other people wanted

   - *shapeshifter*

I want to be selfish
long to be selfish
Give a fuck only about myself

I am not an angel
angels wouldn't
play the martyr
and resent everyone else
for their choices

   - boundaries

I don't like to admit
can't even fathom
that I can hurt other people
and myself
Seeing the flaws
makes me feel
like an ugly monster

- dr. frankenstein

The hardest part for me
is to see and realize
the jagged edges
and soft indentations
that kept me safe
for such a long time
are no longer needed

   - molting

It's easy to blame the mirror
when you don't like the reflection
Chalk it up to a
Not-so-funhouse
distortion

I know who I am
but do I really?

- funhouse mirror

Who is my truest self?
I'm finding her in the spaces

- nice to meet you

Do I love myself?
I don't think
I do as much
as she loves me

Who is she?
Who is me?

   - *whose who*

There is danger in binaries
good vs. evil
There are choices
and there are consequences
If I admit fault
then I am assuming
an identity
that I don't want to accept
I am a good person
I am a bad person

  - *binaries*

I am hurt.
I am enraged.
I am grieving.
I am loved.
I am learning.
I am messy.

- messy black woman

For so long
I doubted
all my feelings
that I constantly
need other people
to let me know
that they're real

For so long
I questioned
my very existence
that I constantly
need other people
to let me know
that I'm real

    - imagine me

AN UNRAVELING

35

We spend our lives unlearning
our basic instincts
Babies are free to cry
free to laugh
free to take up space
free to speak up for their needs
and their autonomy

   - ancient wisdom

All the gratitude
all the positive self-talk
all the feminism
all the empowerment
I shove into my brain
every single day
still wasn't enough
to reach my heart

   - message not delivered

All it takes is
some tequila and a journal
I can do this on my own
slay all the demons

But all this is
Is a zoomed-in mirror
and I have no idea
what to do next

Trying to
therapize myself
is like trying to
tickle myself

It doesn't fucking work

    - diy

Maybe I'm getting
thinner skin
because the world keeps
stripping me
of who I am?

Maybe the layers
have to come off
so I can be
who I'm meant to be?

   - thin skin

Hurting yourself
won't protect you
from being hurt
by others

    - sweet sacrifice

I am not weak
My softness was
made to create
a world in my image

- radical vulnerability

You were never broken
You were always whole
You may not have felt at home
in your body
But you have every right
to feel beautiful and loved

   - a whole human

I keep striving
to get to the next thing

Grow
Grow
Grow

Forgetting that there is
growth in the pause

In the reset
is where the moon
is gone and
preparing to grow again

    - rush rush

You can sleep
when you're dead
But you can also sleep
when you're alive

    - goodnight

I am not a machine
I am a human experiencing
an unraveling
an awakening
Divination

- human being

ALIGNMENT

47

I do a lot
I am a lot
but I have to remember
I am also enough

    - the most

I trust my body
To take care of me
But can she
Trust me
To take care of her?

   - trust

They taught me to
dim my own light
to not hurt someone else's eyes

But the sun doesn't care
how bright it shines
That's what shades are for

 - i gotta wear shades

I don't grow bigger or smaller
I'm just shrouded in darkness sometimes
When I learn to love my darkness
this is when I can truly love myself

- new moon

I don't trust myself
to get it done
even though
I always do

I don't trust myself
to be capable
even though
I always I am

I don't trust myself
to make decisions
even though
I always know

    - trust

Feelings are a sum
of physiological responses
to a stimulus

Love is an action

 - action words

My hand is itching
Someone is going to give me some money
My right eye is jumping
Something good is going to happen
My ears are burning
Someone is talking about me
Is it superstition
Or invitation?
our bodies telling us to trust
What they know to be true

   - *superstitious*

I will unabashedly share my passion
I will unapologetically share my vision
I will irrevocably share my gifts

   - *an oath*

Good dancing
Bad dancing
The world just needs
to dance more

   - dancing queen

A Smile
A Frown
Flipping myself inside out
To share the raw, bloody side of me
My voice
My time
My thread that connects us
To this experience we call life
A drink
A dance
A feeling of being alive
Getting out of this alive

- a list of things I can share with the world

One day I realized
that God was in my self
and when I started
believing in me
I began having
true faith in Her

    - loved her fiercely

Portrait Poem (2023)

I am a loving fighter
I wonder about all the people I'll meet
I hear the stories from those they tried to silence
I see all the warmth and love
From the people around me
I want to be alive
I am a loving fighter

I pretend to be impenetrable
I feel all my feelings lovingly
I touch the lives of those I love
I worry I will disappoint
I cry for the things I still want
I am a loving fighter

I understand how not to understand
I say what I mean with my chest
I dream of a brighter future
I try to do my best
I hope to keep falling in love with myself
I am a loving fighter

ACKNOWLEDGEMENTS

Thank you to my mom and sister. Without y'all, this first book would not exist.

Thank you to Marla and Mary. Your work inspired me to put myself out there.

Thank you to Ms. Bev. You believed in me before I believed in myself.

Thank you to Ms. Gourdine. That assignment in 11th grade launched this book and I didn't even know it at the time.

Thank you to Ayanna. You taught me that my sensitivity was my superpower.

Special shoutout to my friends who gave me feedback.

About the Author

Tayler Simon is a writer, book lover turned bookseller, social worker, and seeker of liberation for all. She comes from southern roots, raised by three generations of love warriors. Tayler wrote her first book in second grade but resisted calling herself a writer until she started her own blog in 2019 and contributed to numerous online publications works on anti-oppression. Through her books, she has made a commitment to radical vulnerability, curiosity, and connection.

Read more at taylersimon.wordpress.com.

www.ingramcontent.com/pod-product-compliance
Lightning Source LLC
Chambersburg PA
CBHW061401160726
47995CB00001B/406